Pig Chinese Horoscope 2025

By

IChingHunFùyǒu FengShuisu

Table of Contents

Introduce

The character of people born in the year of the PIG

People born in this year are wise, trustworthy, kind-hearted, generous, and selfless. It's not a big deal if whoever sees it loves and gets along with others easily. You are cautious, attentive, and brave; try to put your trust in me. You'll know they're so good at doing everything right and never disappointing you. People born in the Year of the Pig are universally adored. People born in this year are born to serve and to give. The majority of people take advantage of this opportunity. Even as they get older, people born in the Year of the Pig don't feel bad about it. People born in the Year of the Pig continue to believe that everyone is born with a good heart. People born in this year are willing to forego their happiness to be good friends who value manners. People who do not know people born in the Year of the Pig well may believe they are unethical. And she enjoys eating chocolate after dinner, which she always overdoes. People born in this year are sensitive, sweet, innocent, affectionate, romantic, and occasionally jealous.

Strength:
People born in the Year of the Pig are gentle, forgiving, and unconcerned about minor issues.

Weaknesses:
People born in this year tend to trust people who are easy to follow and do not have their ideas.

Love:
People born in this year are charming and serious about everything, but they are not as sincere in love as they should be. You like people all over the place, and if you like someone, you'll have to flirt with them. The good-looking kind Please do not approach me. In marriage and love, a woman born in the Year of the Pig outperforms a man. That is, if you meet your true soul mate, you should leave. The young woman will not waste herself or her heart for anyone other than the young pig. Will

not stop there, as a result, finding a serious person can be difficult. Ancient texts say that most women born in the Year of the Pig tend to have a younger partner.

Suitable Career:
People born in this year are charming and serious about everything, but they are not as sincere in love as they should be. You like people all over the place, and if you like someone, you'll have to flirt with them. The good-looking kind Please do not approach me. In marriage and love, a woman born in the Year of the Pig outperforms a man. That is, if you meet your true soul mate, you should leave. The young woman will not waste herself or her heart for anyone other than the young pig. Will not stop there, as a result, finding a serious person can be difficult. Ancient texts say that most women born in the Year of the Pig tend to have a younger partner.

Year of the PIG (Earth) | (1947) & (2007)

"The PIG is in Dhamma Place" is a person born in the year of the PIG at the age of 78 years (1947) and 18 years (2007)

Overview

For young people, since your birth year is a year of direct conflict, this year is another year that you should have a clear picture of every activity before doing it. You must think carefully before doing anything to avoid problems or obstacles that will cause you headaches and heartaches. Therefore, the most important thing in your life this year is patience and saving because your destiny is likely to easily cause conflicts and arguments with others. Even if you are right in some matters, you must endure it. You must reduce your impulsiveness and rashness. Try not to cause trouble. Avoid sources of vices. When you are in a group with friends, some friends may be rash and cause trouble with other groups. Be more careful and quickly distance yourself. Otherwise, you may get caught in the crossfire and get injured or may get caught up in a criminal case.

In addition, while driving or traveling, be careful of accidents. You are likely to mourn for your close elder relatives. At the beginning of the year, you should find an opportunity to pay homage to the annual Tai Sui deity to ask for his protection and to protect you and your family from bad things and experience peace and happiness throughout the year. This is a year that senior people must be very careful. Because the horoscope directly clashes with the Year of the Snake (2025) and also clashes with the God Tai Sui, and inauspicious stars are orbiting to harass the horoscope house, so many aspects of life will not go smoothly. Be careful of unexpected changes. You should always find ways to prevent and prepare in every aspect.

In addition, the senior horoscope owner must conduct himself well. He should not interfere with the affairs of his children and grandchildren. He should take care of his health to be strong. If he goes out or travels far, he should have his children or someone follow him to take care of him for safety. Be careful of arguments and fights. Be careful of unexpected events that will lead to loss of wealth. At the beginning of the year, you should find time to worship the God Tai Sui to ward off bad luck and strengthen your horoscope. This will help ease the burden.

Career and Business

For teenagers, this year, whether it is work or study, you must increase your determination and be extra diligent because the influence of the star Puen Nium causes you to lose focus and be easily moody. Therefore, you must be mindful and not believe in persuasion or challenging words that will lead you down a bad path. You should also not get involved in other people's conflicts because you will be drawn into trouble, especially during the following months when work and study will encounter obstacles and problems: 12th Chinese month (January 5 - February 2), 3rd Chinese month (April 4 - May 4), 6th Chinese month (July 7 - August 6), and 9th Chinese month (October 8 - November 6), which are times to test your determination and patience. This year, if you just follow your friends in their activities, you will lose opportunities.

Especially, do not be a part of friends who like to lead you astray. Be careful not to get hurt. For those who are about to study at university, you should adjust yourself by dividing your time properly. If you do not understand a subject, you can add more time to it. Or try to take extra classes or research on your own online. The months that will be prosperous in both work and education are the 1st Chinese month (February 3 - March 4), the 5th Chinese month (June 5 - July 6), the 7th Chinese month (August 7 - September 6), and the 8th Chinese month (September 7 - October 7).

Financial

This year, you will encounter a loss of wealth. Many incomes have decreased, but expenses have increased. People from both cycles of life should reduce their expenses to balance their incomes so that they do not go into the red and cause trouble. The months when your finances will enter a crisis and unexpected expenses will occur are the 12th Chinese month (January 5 - February 2), the 3rd Chinese month (April 4 - May 4), the 6th Chinese month (July 7 - August 6), and the 9th Chinese month (October 8 - November 6). You must not allow close people to borrow money or guarantee for others. You must not be greedy for other people's wealth, as this will lead to you losing your wealth instead. In addition, you should avoid getting involved in illegal businesses because you may not escape criminal punishment. You should also not gamble or speculate on other matters. The months in which your finances will experience good fortune and become more fluid are the 1st Chinese month (February 3 – March 4), the 5th Chinese month (June 5 – July 6), the 7th Chinese month (August 7 – September 6), and the 8th Chinese month (September 7 – October 7).

Family

The family horoscope of both people in this age group is not smooth because this year is experiencing an unlucky year. In addition, there is a group of bad stars orbiting to look at them, which often affects the health problems and illnesses of family members, unexpected events, valuable property damage or loss, conflicts, and arguments.

And the danger of falling victim to scammers, especially during the months when the family will encounter chaos and suffering, such as the 12th Chinese month (January 5 - February 2), the 3rd Chinese month (April 4 - May 4), the 6th Chinese month (July 7 - August 6), and the 9th Chinese month (October 8 - November 6). What you should be careful of is distancing yourself from some friends who often invite you to vices and joining groups to harass other groups. You have to be careful of the danger of being caught in the middle of a lawsuit. And if you make new friends, be careful of being tricked or slandered, causing damage to you.

In addition, you should be careful of people in the house arguing or having problems with neighbors. You have to be strict and pay attention to the health of the elderly in the house. At the beginning of the year, you should find time to pay respects to the Tai Sui deity to help alleviate bad luck.

Love

For seniors, this year you should not criticize your children or be too picky with them. You will be respected, cared for, and loved as usual. For teenagers, even though this year you are charming and have many close friends of the opposite sex, your mind is usually excited and confident in yourself. However, love during this period is still not sustainable. Do not just listen to sweet words, which make it hard to guess the other person's feelings. If you have problems, you should turn to consult with adults. Being sarcastic or wanting to win is not always positive. The months when love for the horoscope is quite fragile and arguments are easy are the 12th Chinese month (January 5 - February 2), the 3rd Chinese month (April 4 -

May 4), the 6th Chinese month (July 7 - August 6), and the 9th Chinese month (October 8 - November 6). Love that occurs during these times is likely to be deceived. If you cannot control your mind and stop your excitement, you will be too hasty and will regret it later. You should not interfere in other people's love affairs. When visiting entertainment venues, you should know how to protect yourself to be safe and not be fooled into believing that this is the truth.

Health

The health of both horoscopes this year is not good because of the influence of many bad stars that are directly targeting their health. Therefore, both horoscopes should be more careful and take care of their health twice as much because there is a chance of danger to the point of bloodshed and unexpected accidents. Especially in the months that are not favorable to you, which are the 12th Chinese month (January 5 - February 2), the 3rd Chinese month (April 4 - May 4), the 6th Chinese month (July 7 - August 6), and the 9th Chinese month

(October 8 - November 6). During these periods, you should avoid attending funerals. You should be mindful when using tools and machinery. Be careful of mistakes that may cause injury. Be careful when traveling and driving. Also, if you feel sick, see a doctor immediately to nip it in the bud.

Year of the PIG (Wood) | (1959) & (2019)

" The Pigs in the Dharma Center" is a person born in the year of the PIG at the age of 66 years (1959) and 6 years (2019)

Overview

Since your age is directly in conflict with the year of the Snake (2025) and also in conflict with the position of the Tai Sui deity, this year you will be more tired than others. Therefore, please do not be careless. In addition, the inauspicious constellations that are orbiting and influencing the senior horoscope this year often result in unexpected events, accidents, arguments, and loss of property. All activities cannot proceed smoothly. You must increase your awareness and be more careful when walking. When working with tools and machinery or using various equipment, you must be careful of injuries and bleeding. When walking or going up and down stairs, be careful of slipping and falling. In addition, you must be careful of mourning. When driving on the road or driving behind the wheel, do not be careless.

At the beginning of the year, you should find time to worship the Tai Sui deity to ward off bad luck and improve your horoscope. This will help ease the burden and reduce bad luck.

For children aged 6 years old, this year parents and guardians should take care of children of this age carefully while playing sports, jumping, or doing various activities.

When dealing with equipment and tools, including going out to play outside the home it may result in injuries to the point of bleeding. Also, be careful that children's quarrels will spread the conflict to adults. And be careful of illnesses ranging from headaches, fevers, and colds. You should see a doctor immediately. Do not leave it untreated because it may spread to other more serious infectious diseases. Since it is an unlucky year, at the beginning of the year, parents or older relatives should find an opportunity to take the little ones to pay respect to Tai Sui or take the children's clothes to perform a ceremony at a temple or shrine to ask for their help in protecting them from misfortunes, to prevent them from getting sick, and to pray for peace and happiness for the whole family.

Career and Business

This year, if you are thinking of doing any work, you should think carefully before doing it. You should also transfer the work to your children to take over instead. This will help your retirement life be happier. Otherwise, when you fall into an unlucky year, it will be difficult to control conflicts in the department that will arise. There will also be a chance of disagreements with customers or those you have to deal with. What can help when problems arise, you should quickly resolve them. Do not let the problem spread. Especially during the months when your work and business will encounter many obstacles, such as the 12th Chinese month (January 5 - February 2), the 3rd Chinese month (April 4 - May 4), the 6th Chinese month (July 7 - August 6), and the 9th Chinese month (October 8 - November 6), you will encounter serious obstacles and misfortune. When signing various work contracts, you should be more careful to prevent being at a disadvantage or being cheated. In addition, investing should assess your readiness and potential because if you fall for the persuasion to invest, you have a chance to lose more than you earn. You should also take good care of your liquidity and capital. Be careful of subordinates or partners who falsify accounting figures or commit fraud. However, this year, the months in which your work and business will progress and flourish are the 1st Chinese month (February 3 – 4 March 4), the 5th Chinese month (June 5 – July 6), the 7th Chinese month (August 7 –

September 6), and the 8th Chinese month (September 7 – October 7).

Financial

This year's finances are not good. Income is low, expenses are in long queues. Also, be careful of unexpected large expenses that will drain your liquidity. Some people may solve the problem by buying expensive items that they have liked since the beginning of the year to solve the problem of losing money. Also, you are likely to have problems with making wrong decisions at work, causing a shortage of cash flow. Therefore, you must plan your spending well from the beginning of the year. Whatever you can save, you should save it so that you have some left for emergencies. The months when your financial luck is low are the 12th Chinese month (January 5 - February 2), the 3rd Chinese month (April 4 - May 4), the 6th Chinese month (July 7 - August 6), and the 9th Chinese month (October 8 - November 6). You must avoid lending money to others. Also, any guarantees should be suspended. You should not gamble and take risks. You should also avoid investing that is likely to be illegal or immoral. The months in which you will have financial luck are 1st Chinese month (February 3 – March 4), 5th Chinese month (June 5 – July 6), 7th Chinese month (August 7 – September 6), and 8th Chinese month (September 7 – October 7).

Family

This year, your family will lack peace. However, if you can have an auspicious event at home, it will help alleviate the disaster in another way. However, you should be careful about the safety of your family members, especially during the months when your family will face problems from ill-wishers and chaos, such as the 12th Chinese month (January 5 - February 2), the 3rd Chinese month (April 4 - May 4), the 6th Chinese month (July 7 - August 6), and the 9th Chinese month (October 8 - November 6). Be extra careful about illness and the safety of the elderly in the house. Be careful of juniors who cause trouble or trouble. Also, be careful of valuables that are damaged, lost, or stolen. Also, be careful of friends who betray you, find ways to harass you, and slander you. Do not get involved in conflicts between friends.

Love

This year, your love life and your partner's destiny are quite good. In general, you still care for each other well. Although you may have some arguments, they are not a big deal. You just need to be careful during the Chinese 12th month (January 5 - February 2), Chinese 3rd month (April 4 - May 4), Chinese 6th month (July 7 - August 6) and Chinese 9th month (October 8 - November 6). You need to be careful about arguing with your partner or children or people in your home. This will cause you to be neglected and ignored, to the point of not even looking at each other or talking. Therefore, when something happens to someone close to you, if you can compromise, you should compromise. If something is wrong or inappropriate, you should choose your words and find a reason to make them understand each other. Do not use emotions, because this may cause your children to be disrespectful. It is best not to interfere in your children's affairs. You may give advice or help them when they need advice, but avoid using power or giving orders. In addition, avoid going to entertainment venues, which may cause you to get sick. Do not get involved with other people's couples.

Health

The health of both horoscopes this year is not smooth. Young children must be careful of infectious diseases including seasonal epidemics that may spread. In addition, parents must be more careful of children playing naughtily or they will get hurt. As for the older horoscopes, be careful of slipping and falling. New and old illnesses will attack, such as gastritis, liver disease, diabetes, clogged arteries, cerebrovascular problems, and stress. In particular, in the following months you must pay more attention to your health, which are the 12th Chinese month (January 5 - February 2), the 3rd Chinese month (April 4 - May 4), the 6th Chinese month (July 7 - August 6), and the 9th Chinese month (October 8 - November 6), in which you should visit a doctor for a health check-up. You should avoid visiting sick people at night and avoid attending funeral rites or eating at funerals. Be careful of accidents while traveling.

Year of the PIG (Golden) | (1971)

" The Pig in the Barn" is a person born in the year of the PIG at the age of 54 years (1971)

Overview

For this age group, this year is another year that you must be calm in all your work activities. Before speaking or doing anything, you should think carefully. Do not let your emotions be the main factor. Otherwise, you may encounter obstacles and problems that block you, including damages that will follow. This is because your zodiac sign this year has a direct clash with the year of the Snake (2025).

Therefore, problems and irregularities often appear for you to deal with and solve. However, you are lucky that from the middle to the end of the year, you will receive auspicious power from good stars to help you. Your work will progress. Your business will flourish. Therefore, you should be determined to study and develop new skills that are up to date with current events. When the auspicious power comes to your work, you will be able to continue and increase your progress. You will not lose good opportunities. Although at the beginning of the year, you will encounter a storm that harasses your horoscope, if you live your life carefully in every step, use your mindfulness, and make friends with people around you, you will be able to overcome this crisis.

What you should be very careful about this year is your revolving fund. Please take care of and manage your liquidity well. When you have money, save it often so that in an emergency, you will not be in need. In addition, your accounting system must be closely monitored to prevent any loopholes. You must diligently follow up and collect debts when the due date is reached. Be careful that overdue accounts will become bad debts. As for the debts you owe to creditors, you should arrange liquidity to pay them in time. Then you will be able to overcome the crisis. However, when you fall into the unlucky year, at the beginning of the year you should find an opportunity to pay respects to the Tai Sui deity to ward off bad luck so that he will protect you from misfortunes and help alleviate them.

Career and Business

Although your work this year will have conflicts and obstacles in some parts, there will be a good time for expansion. Therefore, you should prepare for additional investment or new investment. Also, be prepared to deal with and have a plan B and B for any problems that may arise. As long as you are determined and know how to develop yourself to keep up with changes, the obstacles that arise will not be able to hinder the progress that will occur. Especially during the months when your work will have a prosperous direction, which are the 1st Chinese month (February 3 - March 4), the 5th Chinese month (June 5 - July 6), the 7th Chinese month (August 7 - September 6), and the 8th Chinese month (September 7 - October 7). However, if it is during the 12th Chinese month (January 5 - February 2), the 3rd Chinese month (April 4 - May 4), the 6th Chinese month (July 7 - August 6), and the 9th Chinese month (October 8 - November 6), which are the periods when the career star is declining. You must be careful of conflicts in the management line. Be careful when signing work contracts or signing legal obligations, you will be deceived and taken advantage of. Also, be careful of being betrayed in the organization and of accounting fraud by insiders. Also, you must review your work or investment carefully because there is a chance of being deceived into causing damage and experiencing losses.

Financial

The finances of this age group are moderate and tend to decline. Regular income from salary or sales of goods or services is decreasing. It is not much better, but it is not affected by a lack of liquidity. However, if you hope for money from gambling, it will be very risky. Do not invest in illegal, immoral, or copyright-infringing businesses. Especially during the months when the financial star is low and be careful of unexpected expenses, such as the 12th Chinese month (January 5 - February 2), the 3rd Chinese month (April 4 - May 4), the 6th Chinese month (July 7 - August 6), and the 9th Chinese month (October 8 - November 6). In addition, do not lend money to others or sign financial guarantees, and do not be greedy. Be careful of falling victim to fraud. The months in which your financial fortune will flow smoothly are the 1st Chinese month (February 3 – March 4), the 5th Chinese month (June 5 – July 6), the 7th Chinese month (August 7 – September 6), and the 8th Chinese month (September 7 – October 7).

Family

This year, the family horoscope of the person will experience both good and bad things. However, if your house can organize an event or have an auspicious event in the house, it will help reduce the negative energy that will affect the family horoscope by more than half. However, if you can't, you should be careful of unexpected accidents in the house or unexpected events that cause loss of property, and health problems for the elderly and family members, especially during the months when the family will encounter chaos, such as the 12th Chinese month (January 5 - February 2), the 3rd Chinese month (April 4 - May 4), the 6th Chinese month (July 7 - August 6), and the 9th Chinese month (October 8 - November 6). The person should not interfere in other people's internal affairs or get involved in conflicts between friends, especially matters related to lawsuits. In addition, be more careful about the safety of both the elderly and young children in the house. Be careful of juniors or servants causing trouble. Also, be careful of valuables being damaged or lost, and be careful of falling victim to scammers.

Love

This year, your love and relationship fate will not be smooth. This is because the zodiac house has found the power of infatuation, causing you to fall into the trap of being charmed by someone who is not your partner. You may also easily behave astray and go astray into vices, or in other words, get carried away with alcohol and women. In particular, the months when the person of your horoscope must be more determined and mindful of your actions are the 12th Chinese month (January 5 – February 2), the 3rd Chinese month (April 4 – May 4), the 6th Chinese month (July 7 – August 6), and the 9th Chinese month (October 8 – November 6). You should avoid any causes that will cause arguments with your partner or lover. Be careful of a third party interfering and causing misunderstandings. In addition, you should not get involved with other people's families. Avoid going to entertainment venues because, in addition to losing money, you may also get sick as a bonus.

Health

This year, the health of the person is not good because of the influence of the evil stars that are focusing on them. It will make you feel unwell. You will often have a headache, a cold, and chills. Sometimes, you may just be sick with a common infectious disease. However, please do not be careless. If you leave it untreated, it may spread to other diseases. Therefore, if you have any abnormal symptoms, you should see a doctor immediately for diagnosis and treatment, especially during the 12th Chinese month (January 5 - February 2), 3rd Chinese month (April 4 - May 4), 6th Chinese month (July 7 - August 6), and 9th Chinese month (October 8 - November 6), when you must take more care of your health. Take care of your hygiene by eating, drinking, and getting enough sleep. Be careful of liver disease, stomach disease, and intestinal disease, and be careful of accidents while using the road.

Year of the PIG (Gold) | (1983)

" The Pig Lives in the Forest" is a person born in the year of the PIG at the age of 42 years (1983)

Overview

The horoscope of those born in the year of the Pig in this age group, because it is a year of conflict (conflict) with the year of the Snake (2025) and the horoscope is still directly clashing with the annual Tai Sui deity, causing your life path to be rather low. Coupled with the inauspicious stars that orbit your zodiac house this year, it will cause anxiety and sadness in the home, illnesses, and diseases to come, and cause obstacles and conflicts. Therefore, in terms of work and business this year, you must do it with caution and mindfulness.

Do not get involved in immoral or illegal businesses because you may not escape punishment and criminal liability. You should also be careful of accidents both during work and while using the road.

Another important thing is that you should be careful of the safety and well-being of your family members. Old and damaged equipment in the home must be checked and replaced frequently, including electrical appliances, gas stoves, or other equipment. If any are found to be damaged, they should be repaired to be in a safe condition. Do not be careless, especially with the health and safety of the elderly because this year you are likely to mourn for your elders. However, it is fortunate that auspicious stars are shining to help amidst the stressful and problematic environment.

However, you have the opportunity to buy expensive property into the home. In addition, starting a new job, entering into a joint venture, and investing in various matters will give a reasonable return. At the beginning of the year, the person should find an opportunity to pay homage to the Tai Sui deity to ask for his protection so that bad luck will be dispelled, and that no illness or misfortune will occur in the family.

Career and Business

This year, the career and business of the person will face a challenging test. If you are not careful enough, you may suffer defeat and be rejected. Therefore, you must be careful in your work and not make mistakes. The team or assistants who help with the work should have a good relationship because if there is a conflict, the work will be interrupted and cause damage. In addition, this year, you must be honest in your business, sell quality products, or provide efficient services. Do not think of taking advantage of consumers. This will help your work find a bright future, especially during the months when your work and business are prosperous, such as the 1st Chinese month (February 3 - March 4), the 5th Chinese month (June 5 - July 6), the 7th Chinese month (August 7 - September 6), and the 8th Chinese month (September 7 - October 7).

However, you should be especially careful during the following months when your career star will change and decline and cause obstacles. Problems occur during the 12th Chinese month (January 5 – February 2), 3rd Chinese month (April 4 – May 4), 6th Chinese month (July 7 – August 6), and 9th Chinese month (October 8 – November 6). During these periods, you should not make new or additional investments because there is a chance of being deceived. You should also be careful of dishonest accounting partners. When signing work contracts, be careful not to be deceived or taken advantage of. When hiring or ordering work, you should document it as evidence and keep proper accounts. If you have problems with government agencies, you will be able to use it as a reference when being investigated. You should also not interfere in other people's work and be careful not to damage your work due to breach of contract.

Financial

This year's overall finances are moderate. Although there is some money from luck, I am afraid that if you get it and want more, it will cause you to lose your wealth. I ask you to spend thriftily and take good care of your liquidity. Most importantly, you should be satisfied only with the wealth that you earn honestly. You should not be greedy and hope for the wealth of others. This will make it easy for you to fall victim to fraud. Another thing you should be careful about is the external economic changes that may affect you. Because if you do not have a strong financial position, you will be affected. Also, this year you should not create debt obligations such as taking out a loan to buy a house or paying for a car. Especially during the following months, you must plan your spending carefully and thoroughly: 12th Chinese Month (January 5 - February 2), 3rd Chinese Month (April 4 - May 4), 6th Chinese Month (July 7 - August 6), and 9th Chinese Month (October 8 - November 6). Do not gamble, lend money, or sign financial guarantees, and do not do illegal or immoral business. The months when your finances flow smoothly are 1st Chinese month (February 3 – March 4), 5th Chinese month (June 5 – July 6), 7th Chinese month (August 7 – September 6), and 8th Chinese month (September 7 – October 7).

Family

This year, the family horoscope of this person is not smooth because the evil stars send inauspicious energy to aim at the horoscope. Therefore, you should be careful of unexpected accidents in the house and should pay close attention to the health of the elders in the house, especially during the 12th Chinese month (January 5 - February 2), the 3rd Chinese month (April 4 - May 4), the 6th Chinese month (July 7 - August 6), and the 9th

Chinese month (October 8 - November 6) when you have to be careful of sad events. There may be a mourning ceremony for an elder relative. For relatives and friends, this year you will meet selfish people. Therefore, in every activity, do not expect anyone to help. Rely on yourself and do your duties to the best of your ability. Do not interfere in the work of others. Also, be careful of some friends who find ways to harass, slander, or harm you. Also, do not get involved in conflicts between friends, especially those that will lead to lawsuits.

Love

This year, you will be moody, and irritable, and sometimes you may speak without thinking, which can easily cause arguments and quarrels with your partner. Arguments will further damage your relationship. Therefore, you must be careful with your words and control your behavior, which may lead to conflicts due to the influence of bad stars. Especially for those who are in a relationship, do not give anyone false hope, as it will only cause more problems. The months when your love life will be easily divided and you will easily quarrel are the 12th Chinese month (January 5 – February 2), the 3rd Chinese month (April 4 – May 4), the 6th Chinese month (July 7 – August 6), and the 9th Chinese month (October 8 – November 6). You should avoid going to entertainment venues because you may get sick. You should also not get involved with other people's families.

Health

Even though your age is still healthy, sometimes the fast-paced life lacks sufficient self-care, drinking alcohol, smoking, and eating indulgently are all factors that undermine and threaten your health in the long run. In addition, there are many bad stars in your horoscope that directly influence your health. Therefore, this year, your health is something that you cannot be careless about. You must be aware and reduce and quit for yourself. You must also be careful about accidents that will cause you to bleed, especially during the 12th Chinese month (January 5 - February 2), 3rd Chinese month (April 4 - May 4), 6th Chinese month (July 7 - August 6), and 9th Chinese month (October 8 - November 6), when you should avoid attending funerals. Be careful when traveling on the road. Be mindful when socializing outside the home. Do not drink too much.

Year of the PIG (Water) | (1995)
" The Traveling Pig" is a person born in the year of the PIG at the age of 30 years (1995)

Overview
For the Pig horoscope of this age, this year, because your birth year is a clash with the Tai Sui deity and the Snake year (2025), along with many evil stars that have spread their influence, causing obstacles and hindrances, making many activities and work unable to proceed smoothly. Therefore, in carrying out various activities, you must not be careless and increase your patience and tolerance for things that affect you in every matter. You must also constantly increase your skills and knowledge that are up to date with the current situation. Increasing your efforts will still have a way for

your work to progress. Business can still expand. Therefore, do not give up and be discouraged because this age is a time of high efficiency. You just need to increase your determination and diligence, and you will be able to overcome various obstacles and problems. However, you should not underestimate the influence of evil stars and clashing powers that affect and focus on the horoscope house.

Especially problems of quarrels, accidents, health problems of the elderly in the house, dangers of mourning for elders, dangers of injuries and bloodshed from unexpected events, unsuccessful work, and business, there will be reasons for losing property and there will often be conflicts and arguments with others. At the beginning of the year, the horoscope should find an opportunity to pay homage to the Tai Sui deity to ward off bad luck. To ask for your help in protecting the person from all evil and misfortunes.

Career and Business

Although this year is your clashing year, the clashing energy in your career will give both positive and negative results. The negative result is that you will often encounter obstacles and problems without exception. The positive result is that the clashing energy will make you aware of changes. You can find opportunities in hidden crises, allowing you to find new paths and channels for your career and business. If you maintain your determination to fight your career and face problems without giving up, the final result will be more positive than negative. The months when your career and business will see a change for the better are the 1st Chinese month (February 3 – March 4), the 5th Chinese month (June 5 – July 6), the 7th Chinese month (August 7 – September 6), and the 8th Chinese month (September 7 – October 7). The first thing you should adjust before opening the door to a new job is your interpersonal skills with people around you. Your actions and words that show humility, along with determination and diligence, will help create a good foundation for your future career.

However, you should be careful during the following months when your work will encounter obstacles and uncertainty, namely, the 12th Chinese month (January 5 – February 2), the 3rd Chinese month (April 4 – May 4), the 6th Chinese month (July 7 – August 6), and the 9th Chinese month (October 8 – November 6). Do not be careless in your work, as this will cause damage. You should always check and use your mindfulness in every step to avoid mistakes. Also, when handling documents, contracts, or any legal transactions, you should go into detail so that you do not have to come back to solve the problems later. You should also not invest or increase your investment during this period.

Financial

This year, your financial horoscope will fall into a state of losing wealth. There will be a reason to lose a large sum of money unexpectedly. Therefore, you should reduce unnecessary luxuries. You should also be careful of losses from investments that lack homework. Also, do not go all out in gambling and trying your luck in the stock market. Do not be greedy for wealth that is not yours. You should manage your financial liquidity well so that you will have enough to spend throughout the year. Most importantly, you should set aside some money for emergency purposes, especially during the months when your finances will be stuck and unexpected expenses will occur, namely the 12th Chinese month (January 5 – February 2), the 3rd Chinese month (April 4 – May 4), the 6th Chinese month (July 7 – August 6), and the 9th Chinese month (October 8 – November 6). During these periods, you should not lend money or guarantee money, gamble, or invest in illegal businesses because you may face criminal charges, be imprisoned, and lose your assets. The months when your finances will flow smoothly are 1st Chinese month (February 3 – March 4), 5th Chinese month (June 5 – July 6), 7th Chinese month (August 7 – September 6), and 8th Chinese month (September 7 – October 7).

Family

This year, the family will have arguments, which will make the person feel irritated and upset. However, there is a way to resolve this conflict by using the principles of kindness and gratitude, which is to be good to the people in the house and take care of the elders in the house. This conflict will be reduced. However, you should be careful during the following months when your family will have chaos and cause a lack of peace, which are the 12th Chinese month (January 5 - February 2), the 3rd Chinese month (April 4 - May 4), the 6th Chinese month (July 7 - August 6), and the 9th Chinese month (October 8 - November 6). You must find a way to prevent accidents from happening at home. Be careful of illnesses of family members, and arguments both inside and outside the house. Be careful of losing valuables or falling victim to scammers. Be careful of subordinates or servants causing problems. Also, do not be close to some friends who like to invite you astray. Be careful of some friends who find ways to bully, slander, or secretly harm you. Causing obstacles affecting people in the home.

Love

This year, you should pay special attention to your relationship at the beginning and end of the year. Give each other more time to reduce the gap of misunderstanding that will lead to conflict. For those who have a family, there will be a third party. If you are a couple, there will be problems of jealousy and sarcasm. The important thing this year is patience and perseverance. Putting yourself in other people's shoes will be a good shield to prevent a rift in your relationship. The months when love is fragile and requires special care are the 12th Chinese month (January 5 - February 2), the 3rd Chinese month (April 4 - May 4), the 6th Chinese month (July 7 - August 6), and the 9th Chinese month (October 8 - November 6). Do not get involved with other couples. Be careful of arguing. Avoid hanging out at entertainment venues. Be careful of sexually transmitted diseases. It will ruin your reputation and your wealth.

Health

Even though your health horoscope is moderate, if this year you feel sick or feel unusual, you should see a doctor for treatment so that it is completely cured. It will not be a big deal. At the beginning of the year, you may have a headache, a cold, allergies, or insomnia. The solution is to take care of your body to be strong and get enough sleep so that you will have immunity to illness. In addition, at the beginning of the year, you should find time to pay respects to the Tai Sui deity to protect you and your family from illness, disease, and various disasters. In particular, the months when you need to pay special attention to your health are the 12th Chinese month (January 5 – February 2), the 3rd Chinese month (April 4 – May 4), the 6th Chinese month (July 7 – August 6), and the 9th Chinese month (October 8 – November 6). Be careful of accidents both at work and while traveling. Also, be careful of infectious diseases, stomach diseases, and food poisoning.

Chinese Astrology Horoscope for Each Month

Month 12 in the Dragon Year (5 Jan 25 - 2 Feb 25)

This month, the Chinese New Year is overcast and your luck is not on your side. Therefore, it is time for you to find an opportunity to make merit, pray to the gods and deities, ask for blessings, and pray to the Tai Sui deity to protect you and your family so that you will have good luck and smoothness in everything. At the beginning of the new year, a good start is for you to set your work direction and plan for the whole year, including your budget. Importantly, you may need to have a plan B and B that can be flexible and adjusted, so that you can be ready for the changing events. As for starting a new job, investing in stocks, and various investments, this is not a good time.

In addition, you should not interfere in other people's problems and work, which will help reduce the suffering and misfortune from the unlucky year.

This month's finances are quite bad. There are a lot of expenses but income has decreased.

There is also a bad omen of losing money. For some people, you can fix the bad omen by buying expensive items that you like from the beginning of the year to reduce bad luck at the beginning of the year. Do not lend money to anyone or be a guarantor. Do not gamble and take risks. Do not invest in illegal or immoral businesses. When signing any documents or contracts, you must read them carefully. Be careful not to be taken advantage of.

Family and travel horoscope You still need to be careful of unexpected dangers and scammers. Be careful of losing or damaging valuables and there may be a chance of mourning for an elder relative. Regarding your relatives, this month you will meet friends who want to take advantage of you.

In terms of love, this month is sweet. Remember these good things. If you don't understand each other one day, think of the day you loved each other.

Your health is not good. Be careful of drinking alcohol, smoking, or getting addicted to vices. Be careful of bronchitis, liver disease, lung disease, and accidents on the road.

Support Days: 2 Jan., 6 Jan., 10 Jan., 14 Jan., 18 Jan., 22 Jan., 26 Jan., 30 Jan.
Lucky Days: 9 Jan., 21 Jan.
Misfortune Days: 12 Jan., 24 Jan.
Bad Days: 3 Jan., 15 Jan., 27 Jan.

Month 1 in the Dragon Year (3 Feb 25 - 4 Mar 25)
This month, there will be an auspicious star orbiting to shine, resulting in smooth work and business for those born in the year of the Pig. You will be able to turn your work into money many times, and what you are waiting for will be fulfilled. What you should do on this occasion is to prioritize your work well, because during this period, there will be many things for you to take care of at the same time. If you prioritize well and finish your work quickly, you will get a lot of work, which means you will receive money quickly.

This month, your financial luck is quite good. If you hope for a windfall, there is a good opportunity to make money during this period. Just don't be greedy or overindulge yourself, and you will have enough liquidity for you to spend on things you like during the New Year.

In terms of work and business, things will be smooth. When the tide is high, you should hurry to scoop it up, work hard to create results, expand sales and income, or push forward the projects you planned to take shape as soon as possible. There will still be a time to receive good returns because you will receive auspicious power to support and promote. Starting a new job, entering into a joint venture, and investing in various projects this month has a bright path.

The family horoscope is peaceful. This month, you will find auspicious power to support you. Inside the house, you will receive good news that will make your face happy. Or there may be criteria to organize an auspicious event. Some people may move into a new house or workplace. Relatives and friends are good. They will find friends to help.

For love, it is a time of closeness and warm love.

In terms of health, even though you are strong, you should not overlook safety. Exercise regularly and eat healthy food.

Support Days: 3 Feb., 7 Feb., 11 Feb., 15 Feb., 19 Feb., 23 Feb., 27 Feb.
Lucky Days: 2 Feb., 14 Feb., 26 Feb.
Misfortune Days: 5 Feb., 17 Feb.
Bad Days: 8 Feb., 20 Feb.

Month 2 in the Dragon Year (5 Mar 25 - 3 Apr 25)

This month, your horoscope is moving towards a friendly line. In addition, auspicious stars are appearing to shine and shine, resulting in businesses and work going on track and being able to move forward to their goals again. On this occasion, what you should do is diligently increase your new skills and knowledge. Do not stop and find ways to expand new income channels to save more money. Cut unnecessary and extravagant expenses and plan your spending well. During the period when money flows in, in addition to dividing it up for savings and spending for yourself and your family, you should also set aside some for future investment. This will ensure that you always have enough to circulate.

In terms of work and business, you will meet a patron. This is a period of opportunity that allows you to do many things, whether it is investing in a new business, expanding branches, or finding new marketing channels, including negotiations on matters that are waiting for an answer. There is a chance that you will receive the expected response.

In terms of collaboration or investment, this opportunity will have a good direction, but you should distribute money fairly to encourage your subordinates, including dividing it up for public benefit, which will be another way to enhance your charisma.

In terms of family, there is a strong patronage. This month, the person will have the opportunity to buy expensive property. Will receive good news or have the opportunity to add family members. Relatives and friends are good. There will be someone who introduces new opportunities as a way to make money for you.

In terms of love, the opposite sex will indulge you. But you should not be too self-centered.

Health horoscope: You will encounter minor illnesses. Please see a doctor immediately. The symptoms will soon be gone. Do not leave it untreated.

Support Days: 3 Mar, 7 Mar., 11 Mar., 15 Mar., 19 Mar., 23 Mar., 27 Mar., 31 Mar.
Lucky Days: 10 Mar, 22 Mar.
Misfortune Days: 1 Mar, 13 Mar., 25 Mar.
Bad Days: 4 Mar, 16 Mar., 28 Mar.

Month 3 in the Dragon Year (4 Apr 25 - 4 May 25) This month, those born in the year of the Pig lack power and do have not enough strength to hold on to, causing you to often miss good opportunities. The important thing you should do during this period is to be flexible, have a backup plan, and have the courage to make decisions so that you do not miss opportunities. In addition, before relying on anyone, it is best to rely on yourself first.

In terms of work, this period will encounter storms. You should not interfere with the work that is under the responsibility of others. You should do your job well. Beware of ill-wishers who secretly saw off the legs of the chair or be accused of harassment and slander. Therefore, you should be careful and check your work carefully before handing it over so that you do not have to face the full problem because your subordinates will cause problems.

In terms of finances, this month is unstable and unstable. Beware of unexpected current expenses that may interfere and cause money to flow out. You should take good care of your liquidity. You should cut unnecessary expenses, especially reducing expenses related to entertainment and various intoxicants. You should think carefully about starting a new job, entering into a joint venture, and investing in various projects because there are still gains and losses.

In terms of family, beware of unexpected events, and dangers from falling victim to scammers, and there is a chance that you will have to mourn for your elders. Relatives are good. If there are obstacles, you will receive support.

As for love, this month is smooth. This is a good opportunity for singles to move forward and ask for love. There will be a good response.

In terms of health, what you should be careful about is accidents while traveling. While using the road during this period, do not be careless.

Support Days: 4 Apr., 8 Apr., 12 Apr., 16 Apr., 20 Apr., 24 Apr., 28 Apr.
Lucky Days: 3 Apr., 15 Apr., 27 Apr.
Misfortune Days: 6 Apr., 18 Apr., 30 Apr.
Bad Days: 9 Apr., 21 Apr.

Month 4 in the Dragon Year (5 May 25 - 4 Jun 25)
This month, those born in the year of the Pig will encounter several evil stars orbiting to harass, causing the orbit to fall and lose its balance. Therefore, the person should be more careful about the safety in the home and the illness of the elderly in the family. Be careful that there will be a chance of mourning. On this occasion, what you should do is to know how to dodge and avoid, and to know how to protect yourself is the best. Try to take care of the people in the home and yourself to be safe. Avoid the cause of the incident or the cause of the conflict with others.

All activities that are in progress cannot be done arbitrarily. You should observe the situation and analyze the incident well before stepping forward.

As for work and business, this period will face a storm. You should plan to prevent the smoothness that will occur. Also, when conducting legal contracts, check the details carefully so that it does not create serious problems later.

In terms of fortune and finance, you must strictly control the measures of saving and closely take care of the liquidity of the money in your pocket. Be careful of leakage points. As for gambling in the stock lottery, you can invest just enough. Being greedy will cause you to lose both the principal and the interest.

As for poor health, You must be careful of stomach diseases, intestinal diseases, heart diseases, and dangers during travel.

Love is moderate, but relatives and friends are not good. There will be arguments because of words and impulsive emotions.

Support Days: 2 May., 6 May., 10 May., 14 May., 18 May., 22 May., 26 May., 30 May.
Lucky Days: 9 May., 21 May.
Misfortune Days: 12 May., 24 May.
Bad Days: 3 May., 15 May., 27 May.

Month 5 in the Dragon Year (5 Jun 25 - 6 Jul 25)
The horoscope of those born in the year of the Pig has passed the storm. This month, the life graph is on the rise. However, there are still some pending problems. Therefore, you should quickly solve them and end them as soon as possible during this period. What you should do now is to prepare all your resources to move forward. During this time and opportunity, diligence and self-development to keep up with the situation will be the main factor in your work.

In addition, you should brainstorm, and analyze your strengths, weaknesses, and future opportunities to improve your work. Because the obstacles you have will be helped until they are resolved. Therefore, you should seize this opportunity to approach the opportunity. Be diligent and persistent in earning and saving money to make it grow. If it is a regular job, you will have the opportunity to create outstanding results. Therefore, remember that the more you do, the more you will get. Therefore, you should be diligent in creating progress. However, this month, collaboration or investment in various fields is not good. Please refrain for now.

Although your financial luck this month is very flexible, your expenses follow suit. Therefore, you must adhere to saving measures first. If you think of investing in short-term speculation, you can do so. However, do not be too heavy-handed, and be careful not to tear your wallet.

In terms of family, there will be good news for family members.

Although your health is strong, be careful of injuries from accidents and dangers from using vehicles on the road.

Love is often full of ups and downs. You must keep your mind steady. Don't be gullible and biased when someone tells you otherwise. Don't be swayed by temporary love at entertainment venues to the point of causing arguments with people at home. If you can avoid going out during this time, it will be good.

Support Days: 3 Jun., 7 Jun., 11 Jun., 15 Jun., 19 Jun., 23 Jun., 27 Jun.
Lucky Days: 2 Jun., 14 Jun., 26 Jun.
Misfortune Days: 5 Jun., 17 Jun., 29 Jun.
Bad Days: 8 Jun., 20 Jun.

Month 6 in the Dragon Year (7 Jul 25 - 6 Aug 25)
This month, the life path of the Pig people has bad stars orbiting in the zodiac house, causing your work and fortune to turn upside down and fall alarmingly. Many activities that were going to proceed were stuck and not smooth as if hit by a storm. Obstacles and problems appear in your work. What you should do during this period is to find a solution for any crisis. Do not let the problem escalate and do not use

emotions or anger to the point of losing your senses. This will make you unable to see the root cause of the problem, which may cause you to find the wrong solution. You should also be careful about problems with your accounts and working capital.

Financial horoscope: This is another month when you will be in a position of losing your wealth. Therefore, you must stop investing in various areas. Do not lend money to others and do not be a guarantor. You should not gamble or take risks. Do not invest in businesses related to illegal or immoral activities.

Family horoscope lacks peace. Be careful of illnesses of family members and be careful of mourning for elders. Relatives should keep their distance during this period because you may be accidentally hit by some friends who caused it.

Love is covered in clouds. Be careful of anger from work and take it out on people at home. It will make the arguments worse. Therefore, please separate work and personal matters. Also, avoid getting involved with other people's spouses.

In terms of health, this month, be careful of hidden diseases and infectious diseases. You must observe for any abnormal symptoms in your body. You should also be careful of dangers while traveling and driving.

Support Days: 1 Jul., 5 Jul., 9 Jul., 13 Jul., 17 Jul., 21 Jul., 25 Jul., 29 Jul.
Lucky Days: 8 Jul., 20 Jul.
Misfortune Days: 11 Jul., 23 Jul.
Bad Days: 2 Jul., 14 Jul., 26 Jul.

Month 7 in the Dragon Year (7 Aug 25 - 6 Sep 25)
This month, the destiny of those born in the year of the Pig will start to stabilize. The path of life during this period is beautiful like a rainbow bridge. In terms of work and business, it is a prosperous time. You should quickly create work, increase sales, and expand both your customer base and production. You

should use this opportunity to strengthen relationships both at the top and bottom levels. This will create friends and reduce enemies, which will help your work go smoothly and progress.

In addition, you should encourage yourself to dare to seize opportunities because good opportunities do not come often. You should hurry to work according to the plan to the fullest. If you are lazy, be careful not to be swept away to the back row. As for starting a new job, joining a joint venture, or investing in various things, this month, if it is new, it will have a good future. You can expect returns.

As for your finances, this month will continue to soar. This is another month when you work hard, you will also earn a lot of money. Therefore, even though you are tired, it is worth the wealth you get.

This month, your family will have good news, but you will also have the misfortune of losing. Therefore, you must be careful of losing valuables and be careful of dangers from scammers. In terms of friends and relatives, during this period, you should be careful with your words and should stay away from friends who like to cause trouble or are hot-tempered.

In terms of love, you must be careful of the other person changing their mind or hesitation. Due to the appearance of a third party, you must be firm and be careful of quarrels over nonsense. Please be patient and calm. Think that a couple must have understanding and trust in each other to get through this crisis.

In terms of health, your body is strong, but don't be careless. You should exercise and eat healthy food.

Support Days: 2 Aug., 6 Aug., 10 Aug., 14 Aug., 18 Aug., 22 Aug., 26 Aug., 30 Aug.
Lucky Days: 1 Aug., 13 Aug., 25 Aug.
Misfortune Days: 4 Aug., 16 Aug., 28 Aug.
Bad Days: 7 Aug., 19 Aug., 31 Aug.

Month 8 in the Dragon Year (7 Sep 25 - 7 Oct 25)
This month falls in the month when the heavens are on your side, so it sends smooth auspicious energy to help, making most problems and obstacles resolved and overcome.

What you should do on this occasion is to be brave but not reckless. Even if you are tired, don't give up. Even though it is a bad year and there are many obstacles, it does not mean that there is no way to progress.

Therefore, under the surrounding pressure, just don't be discouraged or find trouble for yourself. There are still opportunities open for you.

In terms of work, even though there are still problems, if you are determined and diligent in developing yourself, this month you will be able to show results. Therefore, you should push the projects that you planned before into shape and use them to the fullest. Many things in your work are still going smoothly and going according to the goals. However, for starting a new job, investing in shares, and various investments, during this period you should study information and consider the surrounding factors carefully before investing. If you are not sure, it is safer to stop.

Your finances this month are quite good. There is a cash flow from the things you invested and worked hard on, enough to give you a chance to breathe. The liquidity that was lost has been helped, allowing you to circulate money well and have smooth liquidity.

Family is peaceful and there is good support for each other. However, love is not good. There are often arguments and conflicts. During this time, you should behave well, not be easily influenced, and avoid backbiting.

Love will have a positive direction. If you want to date someone, you can tell them you love them.

Health, you are likely to get sick. You should find time to see a doctor for a health check-up and try to eat healthy food and exercise regularly. If you have the opportunity this month, you should make merit, worship Buddha, and worship deities so that illnesses will be alleviated.

Support Days: 3 Sep., 7 Sep., 11 Sep., 15 Sep., 19 Sep., 23 Sep., 27 Sep.
Lucky Days: 6 Sep., 18 Sep., 30 Sep.
Misfortune Days: 9 Sep., 21 Sep.
Bad Days: 12 Sep., 24 Sep.

Month 9 in the Dragon Year (8 Oct 25 - 6 Nov 25)
This month, your horoscope is weak and weak because you have found a bad star moving in to destroy and disturb you. What you should be concerned about is health problems, which will affect both your work and finances. Therefore, what you should pay attention to during this period is to be careful of accidents while traveling and to be careful of sudden illnesses. If you feel anything unusual, you

should see a doctor immediately before it becomes a big problem.

In terms of work and business, during this period, if you encounter obstacles and problems and the old methods of solving them do not work, you should try to find new channels or methods. This will help you and may lead to a new and better path. In addition, if you encounter problems, do not rush to take action because you may encounter trouble. As for investments, this month you should refrain for now.

This month, your financial horoscope is in a state of losing money. You must be careful of unexpected large expenses and should not lend money to others or sign as a guarantor for anyone. Also, do not extend long-term credit like before, so that there will be no complications.

A normal family. Relatives should be careful of some friends who try to stab you in the back. It is better to be careful, but this month you should avoid attending funerals.

For love, there are storms during this period. You must be mindful and control yourself. Do not act in a way that is not proper or deviate. You should control your behavior and speech. Do not interfere with other people's spouses.

Support Days: 1 Oct., 5 Oct., 9 Oct., 13 Oct., 17 Oct., 21 Oct., 25 Oct., 29 Oct.
Lucky Days: 12 Oct., 24 Oct.
Misfortune Days: 3 Oct., 15 Oct., 27 Oct.
Bad Days: 6 Oct., 18 Oct., 30 Oct.

Month 10 in the Dragon Year (7 Nov 25 - 6 Dec 25)

This month, your horoscope is affected by a tragic star, which will affect your career and family life. Therefore, what you should do during this period is:

Prepare your career in terms of both capital and management. Try to plug up any loopholes.

The most important thing is not to do anything beyond your ability and avoid risky investments. Also, be careful about contracts and documents that you need to be more careful about because you might be cheated. During this period, you need to be mindful and patient. Ask for advice from those who know and be diligent in developing skills and knowledge that you don't understand. Then you will see a positive direction for your career.

This month, your finances are likely to leak easily. In addition, your income will decrease but your expenses will increase. Therefore, you should spend thriftily and plan your spending carefully. You should not earn money by taking risks in illegal businesses or importing goods to avoid taxes. Also, do not let people close to you borrow money or be a guarantor for anyone.

In terms of family, there is a chance of losing money due to medical expenses for family members. Be careful of mourning for an elder relative. Regarding relatives and friends, you should keep your distance this month because it will bring problems and hardship.

In terms of health, be careful of gastritis, enteritis, and cystitis. Old illnesses recur and you should be careful of accidents that will cause bloodshed.

Love that this month is still sweet. Those who are single during this period will have someone come to make their hearts waver. For some couples whose love is going well, they may take this good opportunity to walk hand in hand and enter the wedding hall.

Support Days: 2 Nov., 6 Nov., 10 Nov., 14 Nov., 18 Nov., 22 Nov., 26 Nov., 30 Nov.
Lucky Days: 5 Nov., 17 Nov., 29 Nov.
Misfortune Days: 8 Nov., 20 Nov.
Bad Days: 11 Nov., 23 Nov.

Month 11 in the Dragon Year (7 Dec 25 - 4 Jan 26)
This month is considered to have passed the deadly line, allowing you to breathe easier. Although the overall picture has improved, conflicts between individuals remain.
In any case, you will have to use decisive measures and be firm in your position. In addition, you should use this opportunity to be more diligent and hardworking to earn money to compensate for the lost income because your financial outlook this month is bright. Cash flow will flow in both direct and windfall. However, you should not lend money to anyone because you may not get it back.

As for the remaining liquidity, during this period, you can earn more money by expanding channels, expanding work, or investing more, which will yield satisfactory profits. Therefore, you do not have to listen to anyone's objections. You should push your work forward, but you must do it with caution. You should maintain humility. Do not be stubborn, arrogant, or boastful. Because if you act inappropriately, in the future if you need help, you will not see anyone.

In terms of family, you will argue with your neighbor. In any case, please be considerate and help each other so that you can live together happily. Friends and relatives will all cooperate and help well.

Love for singles is very sweet. For those who have a partner, you should make time to meet them closely, which will be more effective than any words or excuses.

For your health, you will experience minor illnesses. If you reduce hot food, it will help you recover faster.

Support Days: 4 Dec., 8 Dec., 12 Dec., 16 Dec., 20 Dec., 24 Dec., 28 Dec.
Lucky Days: 11 Dec., 23 Dec.
Misfortune Days: 2 Dec., 14 Dec., 26 Dec.
Bad Days: 5 Dec., 17 Dec., 29 Dec.

Amulet for The Year of the Pig
"Manjushri Bodhisattva riding a lion"

Those born in the year of the Pig this year should set up and worship the sacred object "Manjushri Maha Bodhisattva riding a lion" to enhance their destiny. Place it on your work desk or cash desk to ask for his mercy to protect you from danger, spread his power to live in peace and happiness, and experience progress and prosperity in your work. She also helps bless your business to be smooth and successful, with money flowing in and increasing, and bringing peace and prosperity to you and your family.

In a chapter on advanced Feng Shui, it is mentioned that the deities who will come down to reside in the Mie Keng (house of destiny) of the year, are deities who can bring both good and bad fortune to you. Therefore, worshiping to enhance your destiny with the deity who comes down to reside in your birth year is considered to have the best results and the most impact on you. This is to rely on the power of that deity to help protect you while your destiny is declining and having bad karma to alleviate it. At the same time, ask for his blessing to help your business and trade go smoothly, as you wish, and bring glory and prosperity to you and your family.

For those born in the year of the Pig this year The horoscope clashes with the position of the guardian deity Tai Sui Yee. There are also many inauspicious stars orbiting to disturb you. Therefore, there will often be obstacles and problems that interfere and cause damage to you. Your career and business may not go as expected. All activities that you will carry out are still things that you should not be careless about. There will often be unexpected injuries and loss of property. You must be careful about confrontations and verbal conflicts. They will cause you suffering and damage.

Because this year, there is a chance that you will easily argue with others. And money will be stuck and lack liquidity.

In addition, you must take care of the health of your elders in the house. Otherwise, you may have to mourn this year. And you should avoid attending funeral rites.

Or visiting patients in the hospital. The relationship with your lover may end due to arguments. And be careful of a third person who comes to destroy your relationship. In terms of health, be careful of falling ill easily without a clear reason. And be careful of accidents on the road.

If you think of resolving the conflicting power and the evil stars that are harassing you, you should set up and worship "Manjushri Bodhisattva riding a lion" to request his power and virtue to help reduce the causes of bad karma and to experience only good fortune and happiness to the person's horoscope. "Manjushri Bodhisattva" or as the Chinese and Thai-Chinese know him as "Phra Mae Bun Chu Pho Sak" who rides a lion, is often pictured at important temples in China next to "Phra Mae Po Eang Pho Sak" or "Phra Samattabhadra

Bodhisattva riding an elephant". She was born before the time of the Buddha and is known as the Bodhisattva who is excellent in wisdom and has a high ability to teach the Dharma. She is determined to help creatures escape from suffering without fear of hardship. Phra Mae Bun Chu rides a majestic lion to subdue the dark powers of evil and make them disappear. The right-hand holds the Yu Yi staff to bestow power, honor, and followers to support the person born in the year of the Pig to bring happiness and peace to themselves and their families.

In addition, those born in the year of the Pig should wear a sacred pendant of "Manjushri Maha Bodhisattva on a lion" around their neck or carry it with them when traveling outside the home, both near and far.

To make the person born in the year of the Pig full of auspicious wealth, to have prosperity and progress in both business and trade and to have a peaceful and happy family throughout the year.

To create better and faster efficiency and effectiveness than before.

Good Direction: Northwest, Southwest, and East
Bad Direction: Southeast
Lucky Colors: Black, Blue, and Gray.
Lucky Times: 03.00 – 06.59, 13.00 – 14.59, 21.00 – 22.59.
Bad Times: 09.00 – 10.59, 15.00 – 16.59.